LABRADOR RETRIEVERS

FAVORITE DOG BREEDS

Dan Lopez

NorwoodHouse Press

Cataloging-in-Publication Data

Names: Lopez, Dan.
Title: Labrador retrievers / Dan Lopez.
Description: Buffalo, NY : Norwood House Press, 2027. | Series: Favorite dog breeds | Includes glossary and index.
Identifiers: ISBN 9781978580350 (pbk.) | ISBN 9781978580367 (library bound) | ISBN 9781978580374 (ebook)
Subjects: LCSH: Labrador retriever--Juvenile literature. | Dog breeds--Juvenile literature.
Classification: LCC SF429.L3 L67 2027 | DDC 636.7527--dc23

Published in 2027 by
Norwood House Press
2544 Clinton Street
Buffalo, NY 14224

Designer: Rhea Magaro
Editor: Tricia Hoffman

Photo credits: Cover, p.1 Parilov/Shutterstock.com; p.2 Tyler Bagwell/Shutterstock.com; p.4 Wikipedia; p.5 Darren William Hall/Shutterstock.com; p.7 sanjagrujic/Shutterstock.com; p.8 el-ka/Shutterstock.com; p.9 Photobox.ks/Shutterstock.com; p.11 Anna Pozzi - Zoophotos/Shutterstock.com; p.13 Jari Hindstroem/Shutterstock.com; p.14 Taisya Korchak/Shutterstock.com; p.15 LightField Studios/Shutterstock.com; p.16 TommyStockProject/Shutterstock.com; p.17 wellphoto/Shutterstock.com; p.19 Matt BT/Shutterstock.com; p.21 Martine_173/Shutterstock.com;

Printed in the United States of America

CPSIA compliance information: Batch #CSNHP27: For further information contact Norwood House Press at 1-800-237-9932.

TABLE OF CONTENTS

Meet the Labrador Retriever

Labrador retrievers, or Labs, are popular pets. Dogs of this **breed** are known for being sturdy, friendly, and **gentle**.

Superman has a pet Lab named Krypto.

What Do Labrador Retrievers Look Like?

Labs are medium-to-large dogs. At the shoulder, they can measure 25 inches (64 centimeters) tall. They can weigh up to 80 pounds (36 kilograms).

This **muscular** dog is built for swimming! It has webbed paws. Its tail is thick at the base and thin at the end, like an otter's.

Labs have stiff, waterproof **coats**. They can be black, yellow, or chocolate brown.

Where Do Labrador Retrievers Come From?

Labs come from Newfoundland and Labrador. It is a cold, northern **province** of Canada. On the icy island of Newfoundland, Labs **retrieved** ducks for hunters. They worked on fishing boats.

In the 1800s, people from England were introduced to Labs. They took the dogs to Europe. They kept breeding Labs. They wanted to make the perfect dogs for hunting.

Do Labrador Retrievers Make Good Pets?

Labs are eager to make friends. They get along well with people and other dogs. Labs love to be a part of family activities. They make great pets that are always ready to play.

These dogs are **easygoing**. They are good for families with kids.

Labs are hardworking and **capable**. They work at schools and hospitals as **therapy dogs**. They make good guide dogs for people who are blind.

Police officers use Labs to find missing people.

Soldiers use them to sniff for bombs.

What Do Labrador Retrievers Need?

Labs are smart and strong. They have lots of energy. For these reasons, puppies need good training. Lessons help **socialize** them and teach them how to behave.

Labs need daily exercise. Being active keeps them healthy and happy.

They love to play fetch. They love to swim!

Glossary

breed (breed): one type or kind of an animal

capable (KAY-puh-buhl): able to do things; skillful

coats (kohts): the hair or fur that covers animals' bodies

easygoing (ee-zee-GOH-ing): relaxed and carefree; not stressed out

gentle (JEN-tuhl): soft and mild; not rough

muscular (MUHS-kyuh-lur): having strong muscles

province (PRAH-vins): a district or region of a country; Canada is made up of provinces like America is made up of states

retrieved (ri-TREEVD): got something and brought it back; dogs that are retrievers find and bring back animals shot by hunters

socialize (SOH-shuh-lize): to teach an animal or a person how to act around others

therapy dogs (THER-uh-pee dawgz): dogs that work in the community to keep people company, reduce their stress, help them do exercises, and help them learn new things

Thinking Questions

1. How does a Lab's body help it swim?
2. What colors can Labrador Retrievers be?
3. Where do Labrador Retrievers come from in the world?
4. What jobs can Labrador Retrievers do?
5. Why is training important for Lab puppies?

Index

About the Author

Dan Lopez is a writer who loves dogs! He has a German shepherd named Hans and an Irish setter named Tam. They love to go for walks in the woods together. Sometimes, they jump in the lake for a swim. Dan lives in Indiana with his wife and three kids.